LIVING ON THE EDGE
STUDY GUIDE

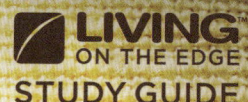

EFFECTIVE PARENTING IN A DEFECTIVE WORLD

CHIP INGRAM

EFFECTIVE PARENTING
IN A DEFECTIVE WORLD

Copyright © 2015 by Living on the Edge and Chip Ingram. All rights reserved. Printed in the U.S.A. For more information go to livingontheedge.org or email info@lote.org.

All rights reserved. No portion of this book may be reproduced, stored in a retrieval system or transmitted in any form or by any means – electronic, mechanical, photocopy, recording, or any other – except for brief quotation in printed reviews, without the prior permission of the publisher.

Scripture quotations marked "NASB" are taken from the New American Standard Bible®. Copyright © 1960, 1962, 1963, 1971, 1972, 1973, 1975, 1977, 1995 by The Lockman Foundation. Used by permission.

Scripture quotations marked "NIV" are taken from the Holy Bible, New International Version®. Copyright © 1973, 1978, 1984 by the International Bible Society. Used by permission of Zondervan Bible Publishing House. All rights reserved. The "NIV" and "New International Version" trademarks are registered in the United States Patent and Trademark Office by International Bible Society. Use of either trademark requires the permission of the International Bible Society.

Scripture quotations marked "TLB" or "The Living Bible" are taken from The Living Bible/Kenneth N. Taylor. – electronic ed. – Wheaton: Tyndale House, 1997, © 1971 by Tyndale House Publishers, Inc. Used by permission. All rights reserved.

Scripture quotations marked "NRSV" are taken from The Holy Bible: New Revised Standard Version/Division of Christian Education of the National Council of Churches of Christ in the United States of America. – Nashville: Thomas Nelson Publishers, © 1989. Used by permission. All rights reserved.

Scripture quotations marked "KJV" are taken from the Holy Bible, King James Version, Cambridge, 1769.

J. B. Phillips, "The New Testament in Modern English", 1962 edition, published by HarperCollins.

Scriptures marked as "(GNT)" are taken from the Good News Translation - Second Edition © 1992 by American Bible Society. Used by permission.

All rights reserved. Printed in the United States of America.

Table of Contents

How to Start Your Own Small Group 4

How to Get the Most Out of This Experience 5

Session 1: How to Raise Positive Kids in a Negative World, Pt. 1 7

Session 2: How to Raise Positive Kids in a Negative World, Pt. 2 15

Session 3: How to Develop Your Child's Full Potential, Pt. 1 23

Session 4: How to Develop Your Child's Full Potential, Pt. 2 31

Session 5: How to Prepare Your Kids to Win Life's Biggest Battles, Pt. 1 39

Session 6: How to Prepare Your Kids to Win Life's Biggest Battles, Pt. 2 47

Session 7: How to Discipline Your Child Effectively, Pt. 1 55

Session 8: How to Discipline Your Child Effectively, Pt. 2 63

Small Group Leader Resources 69

Session Notes 74

Prayer and Praise 81

What's Next? 86

EFFECTIVE PARENTING IN A DEFECTIVE WORLD

How to Start Your Own Small Group

The fact that you are even reading this page says a lot about you. It says that you are either one of those people that has to read everything, or it says you are open to God using you to lead a group.

Leading a small group can sound intimidating, but it really doesn't have to be. Think of it more as gathering a few friends to get to know each other better and to have some discussion around spiritual matters.

Here are a few practical tips to help you get started.

1. PRAY – One of the most important principles of spiritual leadership is to realize you can't do this on your own. No matter how long you've been a Christian or been involved in ministry, you need the power of the Holy Spirit. Lean on Him… He will help you.

2. INVITE SOME FRIENDS – Don't be afraid to ask people to come to your group. You will be surprised how many people are open to a study like this. Whether you have 4 or 14 in your group, it can be a powerful experience. You should probably plan on at least an hour and a half for your group meeting.

3. GET YOUR MATERIALS – You will need to get a DVD of the video teaching by Chip Ingram. You can get the DVD from livingontheedge.org. Also, it will be helpful for each person to have their own study guide. You can also purchase those through the Living on the Edge website.

4. BE PREPARED TO FACILITATE – Just a few minutes a week in preparation can make a huge difference in the group experience. Each week preview the video teaching and review the discussion questions. If you don't think your group can get through all the questions, select the ones that are most relevant to your group.

5. LEARN TO SAY "I DON'T KNOW." – These sessions will spark some lively and spirited discussions. There are lots of different opinions when it comes to parenting. When tough questions come up, it's ok for you to say "I don't know." Take the pressure off. No one expects you to have all the answers.

6. LOVE YOUR GROUP – Maybe the most important thing you bring to the group is your personal care for them. If you will pray for them, encourage them, call them, e-mail them, involve them, and love them, God will be pleased and you will have a lot of fun along the way.

Thank you for your availability. May God bless you as you serve Him by serving others.

How to Get the Most Out of This Experience

These are difficult days in which to raise kids. The world is rapidly changing and the challenges have never been greater for families. The responsibility of raising a child is a sacred stewardship. This challenging and practical series by Chip Ingram will equip you to be an effective parent in a defective world.

Listed below are the segments you will experience each week as well as some hints for getting the most out of this experience. If you are leading the group, you will find some additional help and coaching on pages 70-85.

Take It In (Watch the Video)

It is important for us to get "before God" and submit ourselves to His Truth. During this section you will watch the video teaching by Chip. He will introduce each session with a personal word to the group followed by the teaching portion of the video. At the end of the teaching segment, Chip will wrap up the session and help the group dive into discussion.

A teaching outline with fill-ins is provided for each session. As you follow along, write down questions or insights that you can share during the discussion time.

Even though most of the verses will appear on the screen and in your notes, it is a great idea to bring your own Bible each week. It will allow you to make notes in your own Bible and find other passages that might be relevant to that week's study.

Talk It Over

- **Be involved.** Jump in and share your thoughts. Your ideas are important, and you have a perspective that is unique and can benefit the other group members.

- **Be a good listener.** Value what others are sharing. Seek to really understand the perspective of others in your group and don't be afraid to ask follow up questions.

- **Be Courteous.** People hold strong opinions about parenting. Raising children is very "personal." Spirited discussion is great. Disrespect and attack is not. When there is disagreement, focus on the issue and never turn the discussion into a personal attack.

- **Be focused.** Stay on topic. Help the group explore the subject at hand, and try to save unrelated questions or stories for afterwards.

- **Be careful not to dominate.** Be aware of the amount of talking you are doing in proportion to the rest of the group, and make space for others to speak.

- **Be a learner.** Stay sensitive to what God might be wanting to teach you through the lesson, as well as through what others have to say. Focus more on your own growth rather than making a point or winning an argument.

Live It Out – BIO

BIO is a word that is synonymous with "life." Found in those three simple letters B.I.O., is the key to helping you become the person God wants you to be.

B = Come **Before God** daily – To meet with Him personally through His Word and prayer, to enjoy His presence, receive His direction, and follow His will.

I = Do Life **In Community** weekly – Structuring your week to personally connect in safe relationships that provide love, support, transparency, challenge, and accountability.

O = Be **On Mission** 24/7 – Cultivating a mindset to "live out" Jesus' love for others through acts of sacrifice and service at home, work, play, and church.

ACCELERATE (20 minutes that turn concepts into convictions)

Inspiration comes from hearing God's Word; **motivation** grows by discussing God's Word; **transformation** occurs when you study it for yourself.

If you want to "accelerate" your growth, a short Bible study is provided that you can do at home each week. Our convictions become even stronger when we dig into Scripture and discover truth for ourselves. To help you get the most out of this exercise, consider partnering up with somebody in your group who will also commit to do the assignment this week. Then, after you have each done the assignment, agree to spend 10-15 minutes by phone to share what you learned and what you are applying.

Session 1
How to Raise Positive Kids in a Negative World
Part 1

EFFECTIVE PARENTING IN A DEFECTIVE WORLD

How to Raise Postive Kids in a Negative World, Pt. 1

Take It In (Watch the Video)

> Children are a gift from the LORD;
> _Your greatest joy, greatest pain!_
>
> Psalms 127:3 (NLT)

- Your Child's World is...
  - different than the world you grew up in
  - moving fast   *Character, Christ-likeness.*
  - more evil than previous generations
- A Parent's Challenge is...

  to discover how to help your child navigate this world, stay anchored in God's word, and become a change agent for God's purposes.

- The Question We're All Asking is...

  how do you raise positive kids in a negative world?

4 Principles for Effective Parenting

1. Effective parenting begins with positive

   Positive _Clear cut_ _Objectives_ !

   What you say. what you do.

   > Fathers, don't overcorrect your children or make it difficult for them to obey the commandment. Bring them up with (Christian teaching) in (Christian discipline.)
   > *Physical Lov. of child.*
   > _Father's by Actively Involved._
   >
   > Ephesians 6:4 (Phillips)

   * The Principle of <u>Focus</u> *a clear target.*

   ★ Gods dream Romans 8:29
   ★ Personal dream.

   * God's Dream vs. The Human Dream for Your Child

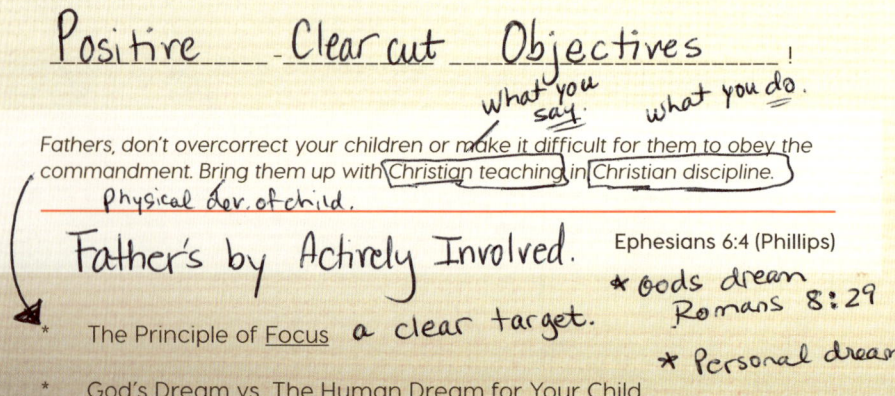

★ Have your kids be different than the culture.

* Be other centered! Be different. Amazing reward!

How to Raise Positive Kids in a Negative World, Pt. 1

2. Effective parenting demands we __practice__ what we __preach__.

Albert Bandora = modeling =

> I am not writing this to shame you, but to warn you, as my dear children. Even though you have ten thousand guardians in Christ, you do not have many fathers, for in Christ Jesus I became your father through the gospel. Therefore I urge you to imitate me. ** mimic, imitate. forgive, do what the Lord does.* 1 Corinthians 4:14-16 (NIV)

* The Principle of Modeling — *"The teacher of your child is you!"*
* "More Is Caught Than Taught" — *Be what you want them to begin.*

Eek! Be Holy like Christ!

Talk It Over

1. What was your parent's goal in parenting? In other words, what was the target they were aiming for in raising you?

   not sure, focus on marriage.

2. Chip talked about the principle of focus. What is one area in your parenting that needs greater focus?

   Focus — Follow the lead of God. Be a good example.

EFFECTIVE PARENTING IN A DEFECTIVE WORLD

3. If your goal truly became your child's "holiness" instead of their "happiness," how would that change your parenting?

I don't focus on trying to make the kids happy. Holiness needs to be the focus.

4. You have to "be" what you want your child to "become." What is one area that you deeply desire to model well for your kids?

Chalkboard – Write something down. How did you do at the end of the day.

Live It Out – B.I.O.

BIO is a word that is synonymous with "life." Found in those three simple letters B.I.O., is the key to helping you become the person God wants you to be.

- B = Come **Before God** daily – To meet with Him personally through His word and prayer to enjoy His presence, receive His direction, and follow His will.

- I = Do Life **In Community** weekly – Structuring your week to personally connect in safe relationships that provide love, support, transparency, challenge, and accountability.

- O = Be **On Mission** 24/7 – Cultivating a mindset to "live out" Jesus' love for others through acts of sacrifice and service at home, work, play, and church.

Come Before God

5. Ephesians 6:4 says, "Fathers, don't overcorrect your children or make it difficult for them to obey the commandment. Bring them up with Christian teaching in Christian discipline." For you as a parent, what does it mean to "bring them up with Christian teaching"? What does that look like practically?

   _____

   _____

   _____

Do Life in Community

6. As you get started in this series, how can this group be an encouragement and support to you in your parenting?

   _____

   _____

   _____

Be On Mission

7. Based on your child's gifting and personality, how could you see God using them in the future?

   _____

   _____

   _____

Accelerate (20 Minutes That Turn Concepts Into Convictions)

Inspiration comes from hearing God's Word; **motivation** grows by discussing God's Word; **transformation** occurs when you study it for yourself.

If you want to "accelerate" your growth, here is an assignment you can do this week. To help you get the most out of this exercise, consider partnering up with somebody in your group who will also commit to do the assignment this week. Then, after you have each done the assignment, agree to spend 10 minutes by phone to share what you learned and what you are applying.

Come Before God

1. In this opening session Chip talked about the need for clear-cut objectives in our parenting. We must get clear about the goal.

   Carefully read the following passage in light of those statements.

   Further, my brothers and sisters, rejoice in the Lord! It is no trouble for me to write the same things to you again, and it is a safeguard for you. Watch out for those dogs, those evildoers, those mutilators of the flesh. For it is we who are the circumcision, we who serve God by his Spirit, who boast in Christ Jesus, and who put no confidence in the flesh – though I myself have reasons for such confidence.

   If someone else thinks they have reasons to put confidence in the flesh, I have more: circumcised on the eighth day, of the people of Israel, of the tribe of Benjamin, a Hebrew of Hebrews; in regard to the law, a Pharisee; as for zeal, persecuting the church; as for righteousness based on the law, faultless.

   But whatever were gains to me I now consider loss for the sake of Christ. What is more, I consider everything a loss because of the surpassing worth of knowing Christ Jesus my Lord, for whose sake I have lost all things. I consider them garbage, that I may gain Christ and be found in him, not having a righteousness of my own that comes from the law, but that which is through faith in Christ—the righteousness that comes from God on the basis of faith. I want to know Christ—yes, to know the power of his resurrection and participation in his sufferings, becoming like him in his death, and so, somehow, attaining to the resurrection from the dead.

   Not that I have already obtained all this, or have already arrived at my goal, but I press on to take hold of that for which Christ Jesus took hold of me. Brothers and sisters, I do not consider myself yet to have taken hold of it. But one thing I do: Forgetting what is behind and straining toward what is ahead, I press on toward the goal to win the prize for which God has called me heavenward in Christ Jesus.

   Phlippians 3:1-14 (NIV)

How to Raise Positive Kids in a Negative World, Pt. 1

2. Look at Paul's credentials in verses 5 and 6. What word or phrase would describe why this would be a significant credential in the world's eyes.

   - Circumcised on eighth day –   ex. religious tradition

   - Hebrew of Hebrews –   _____

   - Pharisee –   _____

   - Zealous –   _____

   - Faultless righteousness –   _____

3. From this passage, what would you say was the clear-cut objective (goal) of Paul's life?

   _____

   _____

   _____

4. In verses 12-14, what are the words that describe Paul's focus?

   _____

   _____

   _____

EFFECTIVE PARENTING IN A DEFECTIVE WORLD

Do Life in Community

5. Who in your life can help you stay focused as a parent? Contact them this week and share with them where you need to focus in your parenting.

_____

_____

_____

Be On Mission

6. Within the overarching goal of your kids becoming like Jesus, write out five specific goals you have for raising your kids.

   1.

   2.

   3.

   4.

   5.

Session 2
How to Raise Positive Kids in a Negative World
Part 2

How to Raise Postive Kids in a Negative World, Pt. 2

Take It In (Watch the Video)

Review from Session 1

1. Effective parenting begins with positive, clear-cut objectives

2. Effective parenting demands we practice what we preach

3. Effective parents build relationships that _____.

> but we were gentle among you, like a mother caring for her little children. We loved you so much that we were delighted to share with you not only the gospel of God but our lives as well, because you had become so dear to us.
>
> 1 Thessalonians 2:7-8 (NIV)

> For you know that we dealt with each of you as a father deals with his own children, encouraging, comforting and urging you to live lives worthy of God, who calls you into his kingdom and glory.
>
> 1 Thessalonians 2:11-12 (NIV)

The Principle of Relationship

Values + Beliefs

RELATIONSHIP

Parent's Lifestyle | Child's Lifestyle

How to Raise Positive Kids in a Negative World, Pt. 2

8 "Keys" That Build Relationships That Bond

1. Unconditional Love
2. Scheduled _____
3. Focused Attention
4. _____ Contact

5. Consistent Communication
6. Meaningful _____
7. _____ Together
8. _____ Together Often

4. Effective parenting requires _____ _____ and _____ _____.

> If we confess our sins, he is faithful and just and will forgive us our sins and purify us from all unrighteousness.
>
> I John 1:9 (NIV)

* The Principle of Process

* 5 Magic Words = _____ _____!

    and _____ _____ _____!

* It's Never Too Late!

17

EFFECTIVE PARENTING IN A DEFECTIVE WORLD

Talk It Over

1. Which of the 8 keys will you commit to work on this coming week? And, 'How' will you put this into practice?

   _____

   _____

   _____

2. The word "encourage" in 1 Thessalonians 2 carries the idea of being someone's biggest cheerleader. In what specific ways can you be a cheerleader for each of your children?

   _____

   _____

   _____

3. Chip said the word "comfort" means to exhort, admonish or help break through a barrier. As you think about your kids right now, is there some particular barrier that they are facing? And, how can you help them get past that barrier?

   _____

   _____

   _____

4. How are you doing at building a strong relationship with your children? During this season, what can you do to strengthen your relationship with your child?

_____

_____

_____

Live It Out – B.I.O.

BIO is a word that is synonymous with "life." Found in those three simple letters B.I.O., is the key to helping you become the person God wants you to be.

- B = Come **Before God** daily – To meet with Him personally through His word and prayer to enjoy His presence, receive His direction, and follow His will.

- I = Do Life **In Community** weekly – Structuring your week to personally connect in safe relationships that provide love, support, transparency, challenge, and accountability.

- O = Be **On Mission** 24/7 – Cultivating a mindset to "live out" Jesus' love for others through acts of sacrifice and service at home, work, play, and church.

Come Before God

5. Paul said, "but we were gentle among you, like a mother caring for her little children. We loved you so much that we were delighted to share with you not only the gospel of God but our lives as well, because you had become so dear to us." – 1 Thessalonians 2:7-8 (NIV). In light of this session on building a strong bond with our kids, what word or phrase most stands out to you? Why?

_____

_____

_____

Do Life in Community

6. What is one fun activity you could do with a friend and their kids that strengthen your relationship with your kids?

_____

_____

_____

Be On Mission

7. Chip talked about being humble enough to say "I'm sorry" and "Please forgive me" to your kids. What words do your kids need to hear more from you?

_____

_____

_____

Accelerate (20 Minutes That Turn Concepts Into Convictions)

Inspiration comes from hearing God's Word; **motivation** grows by discussing God's Word; **transformation** occurs when you study it for yourself.

If you want to "accelerate" your growth, here is an assignment you can do this week. To help you get the most out of this exercise, consider partnering up with somebody in your group who will also commit to do the assignment this week. Then, after you have each done the assignment, agree to spend 10 minutes by phone to share what you learned and what you are applying.

Come Before God

1. Carefully and slowly read the following passage from 1 Thessalonians 2:1-12 (NIV).

How to Raise Positive Kids in a Negative World, Pt. 2

You know, brothers and sisters, that our visit to you was not without results. We had previously suffered and been treated outrageously in Philippi, as you know, but with the help of our God we dared to tell you his gospel in the face of strong opposition. For the appeal we make does not spring from error or impure motives, nor are we trying to trick you. On the contrary, we speak as those approved by God to be entrusted with the gospel. We are not trying to please people but God, who tests our hearts. You know we never used flattery, nor did we put on a mask to cover up greed—God is our witness. We were not looking for praise from people, not from you or anyone else, even though as apostles of Christ we could have asserted our authority. Instead, we were like young children among you. Just as a nursing mother cares for her children, so we cared for you. Because we loved you so much, we were delighted to share with you not only the gospel of God but our lives as well. Surely you remember, brothers and sisters, our toil and hardship; we worked night and day in order not to be a burden to anyone while we preached the gospel of God to you. You are witnesses, and so is God, of how holy, righteous and blameless we were among you who believed. For you know that we dealt with each of you as a father deals with his own children, encouraging, comforting and urging you to live lives worthy of God, who calls you into his kingdom and glory.

---

1 Thessalonians 2:1-12 (NIV)

2. Building strong relationships requires the right heart and motives. From verses 1-6, make a list of statements that are about Paul's purity of heart and motive.

   -
   -
   -
   -

3. From verses 7-12, make a list of the words that are very "relational."

   -
   -
   -

EFFECTIVE PARENTING IN A DEFECTIVE WORLD

4. As Paul talked about discipling these believers in Thessalonica, the metaphor he used was that of parenting. How would you answer the following question... "How is parenting like making disciples?"

_____

_____

_____

Do Life in Community

5. Contact a friend this week and ask them to pray for your relationship with your kids. Then give them some specific things they can pray for.

Be On Mission

6. As you think about being on mission with your kids, what step can you take this week to disciple your child and put 1 Thessalonians 2 into practice?

_____

_____

_____

Session 3
How to Develop Your Child's Full Potential
Part 1

EFFECTIVE PARENTING IN A DEFECTIVE WORLD

How to Develop Your Child's Full Potential, Pt. 1

Take It In (Watch the Video)

God's Dream for Your Child

1. You must understand your child's two primary needs are for _Significance_ and _Security_. ① safe ② Belong.

   - Two questions kids are always asking:

     Do you __love__ me? — body language, actions

     Where are the __boundries__? so important.

   - ★ <u>The Perfect Parent</u>: Genesis 1:27-29; 2:15-17

2. You must recognize your child's primary responsibility is to learn __obedience__. — #priority to learn to obey God, parents!

   > Children, it is your Christian duty to obey your parents, for this is the right thing to do. "Respect your father and mother" is the first commandment that has a promise added: "so that all may go well with you, and you may live a long time in the land."
   >
   > The best channel to have plans go well
   >
   > Ephesians 6:1-3 (GNT)

   - Defining Obedience: Obedience is teaching your child to come __UNDER__ / hear the hearing of your voice.

   > Whoever has my commands and keeps them is the one who loves me. The one who loves me will be loved by my Father, and I too will love them and show myself to them.
   >
   > Calmly with consequences
   >
   > John 14:21 (NIV)

How to Develop Your Child's Full Potential, Pt. 1

3. You must remember, obedience is a __developmental__ process.

   Different ages to teach, think differently

   > Although he was a son, he learned obedience from what he suffered.
   >
   > Hebrews 5:8 (NIV)

   > And Jesus grew in wisdom and stature, and in favor with God and man.
   >
   > _physical spiritual_ Luke 2:52 (NIV)

Spiritual Formation & Mental Development

Who?   Morals   make own good decisions

Rules	Relationship	Reason	Resolve
Age 0-5	Age 6-7	Age 11-12	Age 16-17

Concrete Thinking —(8,9,10)→ Adult Critical Thinking (13,14,15)

Lawrence Kohlbert, The Philosophy of Moral Development: Essays on Moral Development, vol. 1 (San Francisco: Harper and Row, 1981)

Talk It Over

parents and God.

1. Chip said that one of the questions kids answered is "where are the boundaries?" How are you doing at establishing and communicating clear boundaries for your kids? And is there anything you need to do to improve in this area?

   Commander → Instructor → Coach → Consultant
   Goal - learn to obey from the heart - GOD / Parents

EFFECTIVE PARENTING IN A DEFECTIVE WORLD

Boundaries – Henry Cloud.

Tim Hawkins

2. What is your typical response when your kids violate a boundary you have set for them? Is there any adjustment you need to make in how you respond?

I need to step back and be calm.

3. How is it going with teaching your child obedience? What is your biggest challenge with teaching your children immediate obedience?

4. When you think of the chart on Mental Development, how would you say you are doing at communicating appropriately in light of your child's age?

Live It Out – B.I.O.

BIO is a word that is synonymous with "life." Found in those three simple letters B.I.O., is the key to helping you become the person God wants you to be.

- B = Come **Before God** daily – To meet with Him personally through His word and prayer to enjoy His presence, receive His direction, and follow His will.

- I = Do Life **In Community** weekly – Structuring your week to personally connect in safe relationships that provide love, support, transparency, challenge, and accountability.

- O = Be **On Mission** 24/7 – Cultivating a mindset to "live out" Jesus' love for others through acts of sacrifice and service at home, work, play, and church.

Come Before God

5. "Children, obey your parents in the Lord, for this is right. 'Honor your father and mother'—which is the first commandment with a promise—'so that it may go well with you and that you may enjoy long life on the earth.'" Ephesians 6:1-3 (NIV). What does Paul mean when he says to "obey your parents in the Lord"?

_____

_____

_____

Do Life in Community

6. If you were advising parents of pre-schoolers, what would you say to them about teaching their kids to obey?

_____

_____

_____

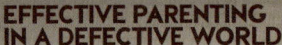

Be On Mission

7. Spend some time as a group praying for your kids. Share specifically how the rest of the group can pray for your kids.

Accelerate (20 Minutes That Turn Concepts Into Convictions)

Inspiration comes from hearing God's Word; **motivation** grows by discussing God's Word; **transformation** occurs when you study it for yourself.

If you want to "accelerate" your growth, here is an assignment you can do this week. To help you get the most out of this exercise, consider partnering up with somebody in your group who will also commit to do the assignment this week. Then, after you have each done the assignment, agree to spend 10 minutes by phone to share what you learned and what you are applying.

Come Before God

1. Carefully read the following passage from 1 Samuel 2:12-17; 23-25:

> Eli's sons were scoundrels; they had no regard for the LORD. Now it was the practice of the priests that, whenever any of the people offered a sacrifice, the priest's servant would come with a three-pronged fork in his hand while the meat was being boiled and would plunge the fork into the pan or kettle or caldron or pot. Whatever the fork brought up the priest would take for himself. This is how they treated all the Israelites who came to Shiloh. But even before the fat was burned, the priest's servant would come and say to the person who was sacrificing, "Give the priest some meat to roast; he won't accept boiled meat from you, but only raw."
>
> If the person said to him, "Let the fat be burned first, and then take whatever you want," the servant would answer, "No, hand it over now; if you don't, I'll take it by force."
>
> This sin of the young men was very great in the LORD's sight, for they were treating the LORD's offering with contempt.
>
> Now Eli, who was very old, heard about everything his sons were doing to all Israel and how they slept with the women who served at the entrance to the tent of meeting. So he said to them, "Why do you do such things? I hear from all the people about these wicked deeds of yours. No, my sons; the report I hear spreading among the LORD's people is not good. If one person sins against another, God may mediate for the offender; but if anyone sins against the LORD, who will intercede for them?" His sons, however, did not listen to their father's rebuke, for it was the LORD's will to put them to death.
>
> 1 Samuel 2:12-17; 23-25 (NIV)

How to Develop Your Child's Full Potential, Pt. 1

2. What are some ways that Eli's sons were disobedient to their dad and to God?

   _____

   _____

   _____

3. How did the disobedience of Eli's sons affect other people? Make a list.

   •

   •

   •

   •

   •

4. Read Ephesians 6:1-3 (NIV), "Children, obey your parents in the Lord, for this is right. 'Honor your father and mother'—which is the first commandment with a promise— 'so that it may go well with you and that you may enjoy long life on the earth.'"

   Why do you think God attaches life going well and long life to our obedience to our parents?

   _____

   _____

   _____

Do Life in Community

5. Have an honest conversation with your spouse or a good friend. Ask them to give you some feedback on how you communicate with your kids and how you can improve.

Be On Mission

6. This week commit to pray every day for the child of one of your friends. You might even consider writing out your prayer and sending it to your friend.

Session 4
How to Develop Your Child's Full Potential
Part 2

How to Develop Your Child's Full Potential, Pt. 2

Take It In (Watch the Video)

God's Dream for Your Child

3. You must remember, obedience is a developmental process.

    - Knowledge Axiom:

        Knowledge + Love + Wisdom = Convictions

        1. <u>Principle of Readiness</u> – Only teach children what they are mentally and emotionally capable of learning.

        2. <u>Principle of Responsibility</u> – Never habitually do for your children what they can do for themselves.

> *Parents, do not treat your children in such a way as to make them angry. Instead, raise them with Christian discipline and instruction.*
>
> Ephesians 6:4 (GNT)

4. You must commit to providing the necessary __resources__ for your child to learn obedience.

> *Hear, O Israel! The LORD is our God, the LORD is one! You shall love the LORD your God with all your heart and with all your soul and with all your might. These words, which I am commanding you today, shall be on your heart. You shall teach them diligently to your sons and shall talk of them when you sit in your house and when you walk by the way and when you lie down and when you rise up. You shall bind them as a sign on your hand and they shall be as frontals on your forehead. You shall write them on the doorposts of your house and on your gates.*
>
> Deuteronomy 6:4-9 (NASB)

Why Great 'A' Executives Get an 'F': Fortune Magazine, Jan 1, 1990

How to Develop Your Child's Full Potential, Pt. 2

- <u>Five Resources Your Children Need from You</u>

FIVE — Teachable

FOUR — Systematic

THREE — Biblical

TWO — Personal

ONE — Doctrinal *TRUTH*
① diff between right & wrong ② Who God is ③ Why he sent Jesus ④ Jesus is fully GOD & fully man, ⑤ The Savior of the World & the way and truth of life.

- <u>A Word Picture</u> = "The Journey of Life"

5. Obedience is achieved when your child has _____

    his/her primary love, submission, and dependency from _____

    to _____ .

- <u>Three Characteristics of Righteous Children</u>

    1. They make wise _____ .

    2. They keep their _____ .

    3. They care genuinely for _____ .

33

Talk It Over

1. How would you say you are doing at giving your kids responsibility? And, what is one area where you can give your kids more responsibility?

   _____

   _____

   _____

2. Chip said "if you want your kids to have great self-esteem, feed them responsibility like vitamins." How do you respond to that statement? What are you doing for your kids that they could do for themselves?

   _____

   _____

   _____

3. What kind of importance do you place on extracurricular activities for your children? How are you doing at applying the Principle of Readiness (only teaching your children what they are mentally and emotionally capable of learning)?

   _____

   _____

   _____

4. What spiritual quality or trait do you want to be sure to infuse into the life of your child? How can you practically accomplish that?

_____

_____

_____

Live It Out – B.I.O.

BIO is a word that is synonymous with "life." Found in those three simple letters B.I.O., is the key to helping you become the person God wants you to be.

- B = Come **Before God** daily – To meet with Him personally through His word and prayer to enjoy His presence, receive His direction, and follow His will.

- I = Do Life **In Community** weekly – Structuring your week to personally connect in safe relationships that provide love, support, transparency, challenge, and accountability.

- O = Be **On Mission** 24/7 – Cultivating a mindset to "live out" Jesus' love for others through acts of sacrifice and service at home, work, play, and church.

Come Before God

5. Read Deuteronomy 6:4-9. As a parent, what most stands out to you from this passage?

_____

_____

_____

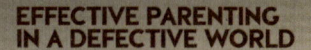

Do Life in Community

6. We live in a culture that puts more emphasis on our kids "doing" than "being." How can you help and support one another in the journey to focus on your child's "being" (heart and character)?

_____

_____

_____

Be On Mission

7. Chip said that one of the qualities of righteous children is that they genuinely care for others. How can you help your kids to have a compassionate heart that cares for others?

_____

_____

_____

Accelerate (20 Minutes That Turn Concepts Into Convictions)

Inspiration comes from hearing God's Word; **motivation** grows by discussing God's Word; **transformation** occurs when you study it for yourself.

If you want to "accelerate" your growth, here is an assignment you can do this week. To help you get the most out of this exercise, consider partnering up with somebody in your group who will also commit to do the assignment this week. Then, after you have each done the assignment, agree to spend 10 minutes by phone to share what you learned and what you are applying.

How to Develop Your Child's Full Potential, Pt. 2

Come Before God

1. Carefully read Deuteronomy 6:3-12 (NIV)

   > *Hear, Israel, and be careful to obey so that it may go well with you and that you may increase greatly in a land flowing with milk and honey, just as the Lord, the God of your ancestors, promised you.*
   >
   > *Hear, O Israel: The Lord our God, the Lord is one. Love the Lord your God with all your heart and with all your soul and with all your strength. These commandments that I give you today are to be on your hearts. Impress them on your children. Talk about them when you sit at home and when you walk along the road, when you lie down and when you get up. Tie them as symbols on your hands and bind them on your foreheads. Write them on the doorframes of your houses and on your gates.*
   >
   > *When the Lord your God brings you into the land he swore to your fathers, to Abraham, Isaac and Jacob, to give you—a land with large, flourishing cities you did not build, houses filled with all kinds of good things you did not provide, wells you did not dig, and vineyards and olive groves you did not plant—then when you eat and are satisfied, be careful that you do not forget the Lord, who brought you out of Egypt, out of the land of slavery.*
   >
   > **Deuteronomy 6:3-12 (NIV)**

2. Go through this passage and underline all the different strategies for helping your kids know, love, and follow God.

3. From this passage, write down some of the spiritual lessons you would like to pass on to your kids.

   _____

   _____

   _____

EFFECTIVE PARENTING IN A DEFECTIVE WORLD

4. From verses 8-9, what is the significance of the following 4 words?

    - Hands –

    - Foreheads –

    - Doorframes –

    - Gates –

Do Life in Community

5. As parents we are the primary influence in the lives of our kids. But we shouldn't be the only influence in their lives. Who else do you know that you want your kids to rub shoulders with? Plan an activity sometime during the next month that will get your kids around somebody else who can be a godly influence.

Be On Mission

6. Spend a few moments praying for each of your kids. Ask God to help your kids love Him with all of their heart, soul, and strength.

Session 5
How to Prepare Your Kids to Win Life's Biggest Battles
Part 1

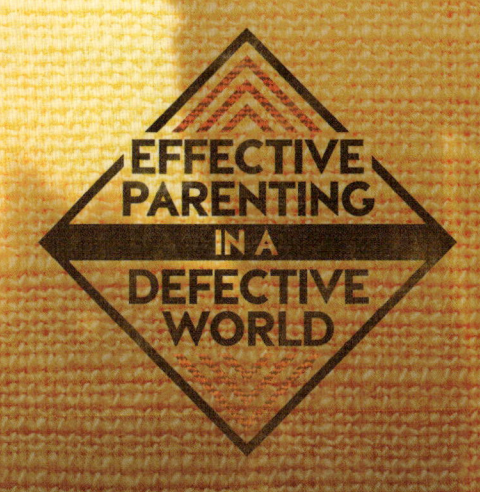

EFFECTIVE PARENTING IN A DEFECTIVE WORLD

EFFECTIVE PARENTING IN A DEFECTIVE WORLD

How to Prepare Your Kids to Win Life's Biggest Battles, Pt. 1

Take It In (Watch the Video)

Introduction: "Five Smooth Stones"

God has been in the business of helping children defeat the "evil giants" in their world for a long time.

1. Teach Them to <u>Suffer</u> Well

    - A Theology of Suffering:

        - Life is hard, but God is good! *[annotation: not blaming others or themselves...]*
        - Life is unjust [not fair], but God is sovereign [in control].
        - Old Testament Roots – Joseph (Genesis 37-50)
        - New Testament Command – 1 Peter 2:21-23

    Application: Help your child <u>grow</u> <u>through</u> <u>suffering</u>.

    Life Message: Suffering is <u>necessary & normal</u>.

2. Teach Them to <u>Work</u> "Unto the Lord"

    - A Theology of Work:

        - Work is a "calling" not a job.
        - All work is sacred.
        - Our work is to flow from God's unique design and purpose for our lives.
        - Work is for one audience; the "audience of one."
        - Old Testament Roots – Genesis 2:15
        - New Testament Command – Colossians 3:23

    Application: Help your child discover "God's calling" for their life so they can impact their world and beyond.

    Life Message: You were _____ to work.

How to Prepare Your Kids to Win Life's Biggest Battles, Pt. 1

3. Teach Them to <u>Manage</u> Their Lives Wisely

   - A Theology of Stewardship:
     - God owns everything.
     - God has entrusted us with "things" to manage for Him. (time, talent, treasure)
     - God expects a positive return on His investment.
     - God will hold you accountable.
     - God wants you to share in His joy.
     - Old Testament Roots – Genesis 1:26-28
     - New Testament Command – Matthew 25:14-30

   Application: Help your child to become _____ in the "little things" – Luke 16:10

   Life Message: Your life is a _____ stewardship.

Talk It Over

1. When you were growing up, what was your family's attitude toward money and stewardship?

   _____

   _____

   _____

2. What adjustment or change do you need to make in your finances in order to model good stewardship for your kids?

   _____

   _____

   _____

EFFECTIVE PARENTING IN A DEFECTIVE WORLD

3. As a group, brainstorm ideas on practical ways that you can teach your kids to be good financial stewards and managers of what God has entrusted to them.

   _____

   _____

   _____

4. Chip said that our work should flow from God's unique design and purpose. Share one or two things that God has uniquely designed your kids to do well. How can you nurture those qualities?

   _____

   _____

   _____

Live It Out – B.I.O.

BIO is a word that is synonymous with "life." Found in those three simple letters B.I.O., is the key to helping you become the person God wants you to be.

- B = Come **Before God** daily – To meet with Him personally through His word and prayer to enjoy His presence, receive His direction, and follow His will.

- I = Do Life **In Community** weekly – Structuring your week to personally connect in safe relationships that provide love, support, transparency, challenge, and accountability.

- O = Be **On Mission** 24/7 – Cultivating a mindset to "live out" Jesus' love for others through acts of sacrifice and service at home, work, play, and church.

How to Prepare Your Kids to Win Life's Biggest Battles, Pt. 1

Come Before God

5. Colossians 3:23 (NASB) says, "Whatever you do, do your work heartily, as for the Lord rather than for men,"

   How can we teach our children to have a strong work ethic?

   _____

   _____

   _____

Do Life in Community

6. It is not in our child's best interest for us to rescue them from everything hard and painful. Share a hard and painful experience from your life that God used to grow you.

   _____

   _____

   _____

Be On Mission

7. How does suffering well help us reach our friends for Christ?

   _____

   _____

   _____

EFFECTIVE PARENTING IN A DEFECTIVE WORLD

Accelerate (20 Minutes That Turn Concepts Into Convictions)

Inspiration comes from hearing God's Word; **motivation** grows by discussing God's Word; **transformation** occurs when you study it for yourself.

If you want to "accelerate" your growth, here is an assignment you can do this week. To help you get the most out of this exercise, consider partnering up with somebody in your group who will also commit to do the assignment this week. Then, after you have each done the assignment, agree to spend 10 minutes by phone to share what you learned and what you are applying.

Come Before God

1. Carefully read the following passage from Genesis 50:15-21 (NIV).

   > *When Joseph's brothers saw that their father was dead, they said, "What if Joseph holds a grudge against us and pays us back for all the wrongs we did to him?" So they sent word to Joseph, saying, "Your father left these instructions before he died: 'This is what you are to say to Joseph: I ask you to forgive your brothers the sins and the wrongs they committed in treating you so badly.' Now please forgive the sins of the servants of the God of your father." When their message came to him, Joseph wept.*
   >
   > *His brothers then came and threw themselves down before him. "We are your slaves," they said.*
   >
   > *But Joseph said to them, "Don't be afraid. Am I in the place of God? You intended to harm me, but God intended it for good to accomplish what is now being done, the saving of many lives. So then, don't be afraid. I will provide for you and your children." And he reassured them and spoke kindly to them.*
   >
   > Genesis 50:15-21 (NIV)

2. Take some extended time and read the story of Joseph, which is recorded in Genesis 37-50. As you reflect on Joseph's story, what most stands out to you about his life and how he handled suffering?

   _____

   _____

   _____

How to Prepare Your Kids to Win Life's Biggest Battles, Pt. 1

3. At the end of Genesis 50:17, why do you think Joseph weeps when his brothers spoke to him?

   _____

   _____

   _____

4. From Joseph's response in Genesis 50:19-21, what are some lessons we can learn about suffering well?

   .

   .

   .

   .

   .

Do Life in Community

5. Write a personal note of encouragement to a friend that is going through a season of suffering.

Be On Mission

6. Who is somebody that you know that is going through a time of suffering? Have a time of prayer with your kids on behalf of this person. Use it also as a teachable moment with your kids.

Session 6
How to Prepare Your Kids to Win Life's Biggest Battles
Part 2

EFFECTIVE PARENTING IN A DEFECTIVE WORLD

How to Prepare Your Kids to Win Life's Biggest Battles, Pt. 2

Take It In (Watch the Video)

Introduction: "Five Smooth Stones"

4. Teach Them to Make _____ Decisions.

    - A Theology of Holiness:
        - God is high, holy, "totally other."
        - God is absolute Truth.
        - God's Word defines absolute Truth.
        - God's law (morals) is for our protection.
        - God's ultimate aim is to make us holy.
        - Old Testament Roots – Exodus 3:5-6
        - New Testament Command – 1 Peter 1:15-16

    Application: Help your child think _____ and critically to develop personal _____ and character.

    Life Message: _____ is the only way to get God's best for your life.

5. Teach Them to Live <u>Grace-Filled</u> Lives.

    - A Theology of Grace:
        - Grace is the unmerited and unconditional love of God toward us.
        - Grace is free to us, but costly to God.
        - The cross is God's greatest act of grace.
        - Salvation is a free gift from God.

How to Prepare Your Kids to Win Life's Biggest Battles, Pt. 2

- Grace must be received. (i.e. faith)
- Grace produces gratitude toward God, and love toward others.
- Old Testament Roots – Genesis 3:21
- New Testament Command – Ephesians 2:8-10; 1 Peter 1:13

Application: Help your child realize that _____ is never final with God.

Life Message: You were created to _____ grace and to give grace.

Talk It Over

1. As you think about your kids and their stage of development, what are some practical steps you can take to help them think critically and biblically?

   _____

   _____

   _____

2. Chip encouraged us to monitor what goes into our child's mind. How are you doing with this and what steps should you consider in order to do this better?

   _____

   _____

   _____

EFFECTIVE PARENTING IN A DEFECTIVE WORLD

3. Share at least one "conviction" you want your kids to have and "own" for themselves?

   _____

   _____

   _____

4. Chip said that your child's ability to make wise decisions is rooted in a theology of God as "holy." If you had to sit down and explain God's holiness to your kids, what would you say?

   _____

   _____

   _____

Live It Out – B.I.O.

BIO is a word that is synonymous with "life." Found in those three simple letters B.I.O., is the key to helping you become the person God wants you to be.

- B = Come **Before God** daily – To meet with Him personally through His word and prayer to enjoy His presence, receive His direction, and follow His will.

- I = Do Life **In Community** weekly – Structuring your week to personally connect in safe relationships that provide love, support, transparency, challenge, and accountability.

- O = Be **On Mission** 24/7 – Cultivating a mindset to "live out" Jesus' love for others through acts of sacrifice and service at home, work, play, and church.

How to Prepare Your Kids to Win Life's Biggest Battles, Pt. 2

Come Before God

5. Ephesians 2:4-7 (NLT) says, "But God is so rich in mercy, and He loved us so much, that even though we were dead because of our sins, He gave us life when He raised Christ from the dead. (It is only by God's grace that you have been saved!) For He raised us from the dead along with Christ and seated us with Him in the heavenly realms because we are united with Christ Jesus. So God can point to us in all future ages as examples of the incredible wealth of His grace and kindness toward us, as shown in all He has done for us who are united with Christ Jesus."

    As you think about helping your kids understand grace, what insight about grace most stands out to you from this passage?

    _____

    _____

    _____

Do Life in Community

6. Of these 5 lessons to pass on to our kids...

    - Teach them to suffer well

    - Teach them to work unto the Lord

    - Teach them to manage their lives wisely

    - Teach them to make wise decisions

    - Teach them to live grace-filled lives

    which one do you most need to work on? Take some time right now to pray for one another.

    _____

    _____

    _____

EFFECTIVE PARENTING IN A DEFECTIVE WORLD

Be On Mission

7. One of the ways our kids learn that failure is not final is by receiving "grace" from us. How can you get better at showing grace to your kids?

_____

_____

_____

Accelerate (20 Minutes That Turn Concepts Into Convictions)

Inspiration comes from hearing God's Word; **motivation** grows by discussing God's Word; **transformation** occurs when you study it for yourself.

If you want to "accelerate" your growth, here is an assignment you can do this week. To help you get the most out of this exercise, consider partnering up with somebody in your group who will also commit to do the assignment this week. Then, after you have each done the assignment, agree to spend 10 minutes by phone to share what you learned and what you are applying.

Come Before God

1. Carefully read the following passage from 2 Samuel 9 (NIV):

> *David asked, "Is there anyone still left of the house of Saul to whom I can show kindness for Jonathan's sake?"*
>
> *Now there was a servant of Saul's household named Ziba. They summoned him to appear before David, and the king said to him, "Are you Ziba?"*
>
> *"At your service," he replied.*
>
> *The king asked, "Is there no one still alive from the house of Saul to whom I can show God's kindness?"*
>
> *Ziba answered the king, "There is still a son of Jonathan; he is lame in both feet."*
>
> *"Where is he?" the king asked.*
>
> *Ziba answered, "He is at the house of Makir son of Ammiel in Lo Debar."*
>
> *So King David had him brought from Lo Debar, from the house of Makir son of Ammiel.*
>
> *When Mephibosheth son of Jonathan, the son of Saul, came to David, he bowed down to pay him honor.*

How to Prepare Your Kids to Win Life's Biggest Battles, Pt. 2

> David said, "Mephibosheth!"
>
> "At your service," he replied.
>
> "Don't be afraid," David said to him, "for I will surely show you kindness for the sake of your father Jonathan. I will restore to you all the land that belonged to your grandfather Saul, and you will always eat at my table."
>
> Mephibosheth bowed down and said, "What is your servant, that you should notice a dead dog like me?"
>
> Then the king summoned Ziba, Saul's steward, and said to him, "I have given your master's grandson everything that belonged to Saul and his family. You and your sons and your servants are to farm the land for him and bring in the crops, so that your master's grandson may be provided for. And Mephibosheth, grandson of your master, will always eat at my table." (Now Ziba had fifteen sons and twenty servants.)
>
> Then Ziba said to the king, "Your servant will do whatever my lord the king commands his servant to do." So Mephibosheth ate at David's table like one of the king's sons.
>
> Mephibosheth had a young son named Mika, and all the members of Ziba's household were servants of Mephibosheth. And Mephibosheth lived in Jerusalem, because he always ate at the king's table; he was lame in both feet.
>
> 2 Samuel 9 (NIV)

2. How did Mephibosheth become crippled? See 2 Samuel 4:4.

   _____

   _____

   _____

3. Read verses 6-8 again. What do you think was going on inside of Mephibosheth when he was brought before King David?

   _____

   _____

   _____

4. Go through this passage and underline every word or action of David that represents "grace."

5. Read through Ephesians 1:3-14 and make a list of all the blessings (grace) we have received in Christ.

_____

_____

_____

Do Life in Community

6. Who is somebody who has shown you grace in the past? Make it a point to reach out to them and thank them for demonstrating God's grace to you.

Be On Mission

7. Who do you know in your neighborhood or church that could use a little "grace"? Involve your kids in helping you extend some "lavish" grace on that person.

Session 7
How to Discipline Your Child Effectively
Part 1

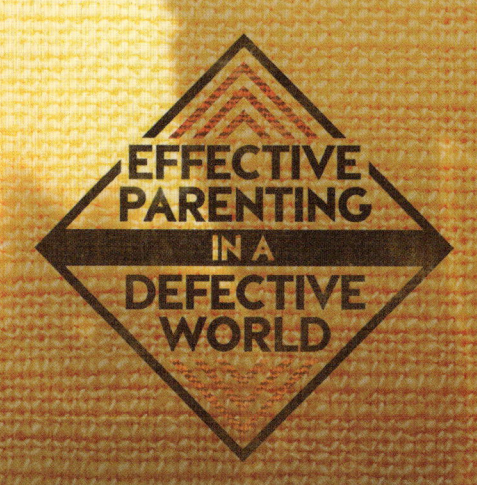

EFFECTIVE PARENTING IN A DEFECTIVE WORLD

How to Discipline Your Child Effectively, Pt. 1

Take It In (Watch the Video)

Two Case Studies

Case Study #1 – The Rueben Hill Minnesota Report

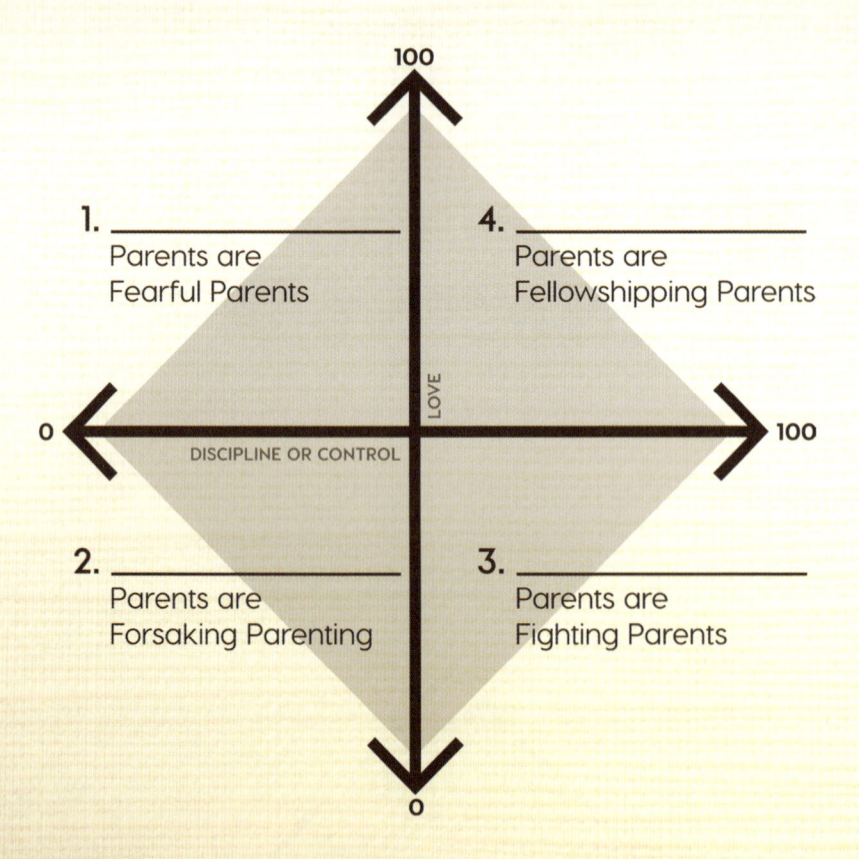

```
                        100
                         ↑
        1. _____    4. _____
        Parents are         Parents are
        Fearful Parents     Fellowshipping Parents

                        LOVE
    0 ←──────────── DISCIPLINE OR CONTROL ────────────→ 100

        2. _____    3. _____
        Parents are         Parents are
        Forsaking Parenting Fighting Parents

                         ↓
                         0
```

Reuben Hills' research as presented by Dr. Richard Meier in a seminar on parenting, MinirthMeier Clinic, Dallas TX, 1988

Summary – The **Authoritative** parent, who gives <u>high support</u> (love) and <u>high control</u> (discipline), typically produced children with **high self esteem, good coping skills** and a **positive relationship with parents.**

How to Discipline Your Child Effectively, Pt. 1

Case Study #2 – Hebrews 12 – Christians AD 66-70

> In your struggle against sin, you have not yet resisted to the point of shedding your blood. And have you completely forgotten this word of encouragement that addresses you as a father addresses his son? It says,
>
>> "My son, do not make light of the Lord's discipline,
>>   and do not lose heart when he rebukes you,
>> because the Lord disciplines the one he loves,
>>   and He chastens everyone he accepts as his son."
>
> Endure hardship as discipline; God is treating you as His children. For what children are not disciplined by their father? If you are not disciplined—and everyone undergoes discipline—then you are not legitimate, not true sons and daughters at all. Moreover, we have all had human fathers who disciplined us and we respected them for it. How much more should we submit to the Father of spirits and live! They disciplined us for a little while as they thought best; but God disciplines us for our good, in order that we may share in His holiness.
>
> No discipline seems pleasant at the time, but painful. Later on, however, it produces a harvest of righteousness and peace for those who have been trained by it.
>
> Hebrews 12:4-11 (NIV)

Summary – **Discipline** is teaching **obedience** to God and His Word through <u>consistent consequences</u> (actions) and <u>clear instructions</u> (words) in an **atmosphere of love**.

Five Characteristics of Discipline:

1. The necessity of discipline – To Deter Destruction (vs 4)

2. The means of discipline – The _____ and _____ (vs 5)

3. The motive in discipline – To Express Love (vs 6-9)

4. The goal of discipline – To Teach _____ (vs 9)

5. The result of discipline – Short-term Pain and Long-term Gain (vs 10-11)

EFFECTIVE PARENTING IN A DEFECTIVE WORLD

Knowing the Difference Between Punishment and Discipline

	Punishment	Discipline
Purpose	To Inflict Penalty for An Offense	To Train for Correction and Maturity
Focus	Past Misdeeds	Future Correct Acts
Attitude	Hostility and Frustration on the Part of the Parent	Love and Concern on the Part of the Parent
Resulting Emotion in the Child	Fear and Guilt	Security

Talk It Over

1. Of the other three styles... permissive, neglectful, and authoritarian which one are you most likely to fall into in your parenting? And what does that look like practically?

   _____

   _____

   _____

2. As you look back to your childhood, how would you describe your parent's approach to discipline?

   _____

   _____

   _____

How to Discipline Your Child Effectively, Pt. 1

3. As you look at that passage in Hebrews 12:4-11, what are some of the qualities that describe God's approach to discipline?

_____

_____

_____

4. For you personally, what is your greatest challenge in disciplining your kids?

- Being passive?
- Not being consistent?
- Disciplining out of anger?
- Not having clear consequences?
- Giving in to your kids?
- Something else?

Live It Out – B.I.O.

BIO is a word that is synonymous with "life." Found in those three simple letters B.I.O., is the key to helping you become the person God wants you to be.

- B = Come **Before God** daily – To meet with Him personally through His word and prayer to enjoy His presence, receive His direction, and follow His will.

- I = Do Life **In Community** weekly – Structuring your week to personally connect in safe relationships that provide love, support, transparency, challenge, and accountability.

- O = Be **On Mission** 24/7 – Cultivating a mindset to "live out" Jesus' love for others through acts of sacrifice and service at home, work, play, and church.

EFFECTIVE PARENTING IN A DEFECTIVE WORLD

Come Before God

5. Speaking about our earthly fathers, Hebrews 12:10 says, "They disciplined us for a little while as they thought best; but God disciplines us for our good, in order that we may share in his holiness."

   How does God's discipline in our lives allow us to share in His holiness?

   _____

   _____

   _____

Do Life in Community

6. Proverbs 11:14 (NLT) says, "Without wise leadership, a nation falls; there is safety in having many advisers."

   Share a situation that you are facing with your child and let those in your group give you their counsel and advice.

   _____

   _____

   _____

Be On Mission

7. Hebrews 12:11 says that discipline produces a harvest of righteousness and peace. Think ahead to the time when your kids are grown. What is the hope and longing you have as far as what discipline would have produced in their lives?

   _____

   _____

   _____

How to Discipline Your Child Effectively, Pt. 1

Accelerate (20 Minutes That Turn Concepts Into Convictions)

Inspiration comes from hearing God's Word; **motivation** grows by discussing God's Word; **transformation** occurs when you study it for yourself.

If you want to "accelerate" your growth, here is an assignment you can do this week. To help you get the most out of this exercise, consider partnering up with somebody in your group who will also commit to do the assignment this week. Then, after you have each done the assignment, agree to spend 10 minutes by phone to share what you learned and what you are applying.

Come Before God

1. Carefully read the following passage from Hebrews 12:1-11 (NIV):

   Therefore, since we are surrounded by such a great cloud of witnesses, let us throw off everything that hinders and the sin that so easily entangles. And let us run with perseverance the race marked out for us, fixing our eyes on Jesus, the pioneer and perfecter of faith. For the joy set before him he endured the cross, scorning its shame, and sat down at the right hand of the throne of God. Consider him who endured such opposition from sinners, so that you will not grow weary and lose heart.

   God Disciplines His Children

   In your struggle against sin, you have not yet resisted to the point of shedding your blood. And have you completely forgotten this word of encouragement that addresses you as a father addresses his son? It says,

   > *"My son, do not make light of the Lord's discipline,*
   >   *and do not lose heart when he rebukes you,*
   > *because the Lord disciplines the one he loves,*
   >   *and he chastens everyone he accepts as his son."*

   Endure hardship as discipline; God is treating you as his children. For what children are not disciplined by their father? If you are not disciplined—and everyone undergoes discipline—then you are not legitimate, not true sons and daughters at all. Moreover, we have all had human fathers who disciplined us and we respected them for it. How much more should we submit to the Father of spirits and live! They disciplined us for a little while as they thought best; but God disciplines us for our good, in order that we may share in his holiness. No discipline seems pleasant at the time, but painful. Later on, however, it produces a harvest of righteousness and peace for those who have been trained by it.

   Hebrews 12:1-11 (NIV)

EFFECTIVE PARENTING IN A DEFECTIVE WORLD

2. When it comes to disciplining our kids, it is a marathon, not a sprint. What principles in Hebrews 12:1-3 can you find that help you in taking a long term (marathon) approach to parenting?

   _____

   _____

   _____

3. Go through this passage and underline every word that describes God's discipline. Spend some time praying and asking God to let your discipline reflect the same heart and qualities.

4. Speaking about our earthly fathers, Hebrews 12:10 says, "They disciplined us for a little while as they thought best; but God disciplines us for our good, in order that we may share in His holiness."

   How does God's discipline in our lives allow us to share in His holiness?

   _____

   _____

   _____

Do Life in Community

5. Have a conversation with your spouse or a close friend this week about the issue of discipline. Share with them how they can encourage you and hold you accountable when it comes to disciplining your kids.

Be On Mission

6. Hebrews 12:11 says that discipline, "produces a harvest of righteousness and peace for those who have been trained by it." Reflect for a few moments on what a harvest of righteousness and peace would mean for your child. Then, complete the following statement…

   Dear God, my hope and dream for the discipline of my kids is that it would

   produce in them… _____

Session 8
How to Discipline Your Child Effectively
Part 2

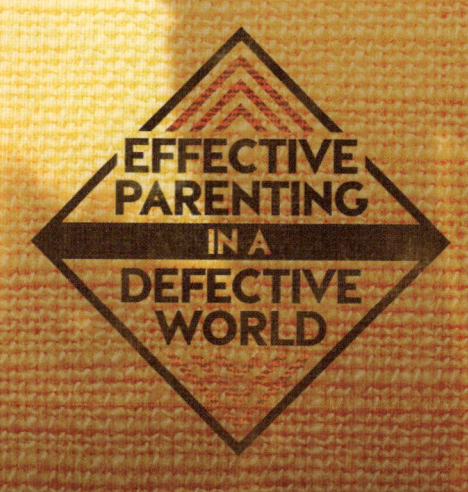

EFFECTIVE PARENTING IN A DEFECTIVE WORLD

How to Discipline Your Child Effectively, Pt. 2

Take It In (Watch the Video)

Two Key Biblical Concepts

1. Actions = Consistent Consequences - Proverbs 13:24, 22:15

    Seven Steps to Discipline:

    1. Clear _____
    2. Establish Responsibility
    3. Avoid _____
    4. Communicate Grief
    5. Flick the _____
    6. Sincere Repentance
    7. Unconditional _____

2. Words = Clear Instructions - Proverbs 3:11-12

    Four Ways to Use Words to Bring About Correction:

    1. Say "No" Firmly
    2. Clear Warning of Consequences
    3. Use Contracts
    4. Use Consequences

Practical Tips for Balanced Parenting

- Avoid the Pitfalls
    - The Screaming Parent
    - The All Talk Parent
    - The Abusive Parent
    - The "Close-lipped" Parent
    - The Light Bulb Parent

How to Discipline Your Child Effectively, Pt. 2

- Develop a Game plan
    1. Identify the top two behavior problems.
    2. Honestly identify your parenting pattern.
    3. Have a family conference.
    4. Set goals together.

Talk It Over

1. Of the Seven Steps to Discipline, which of the seven do you do well and which one do you need to work on?

    _____

    _____

    _____

2. Sin is not primarily about behavior, it is about relationship. How should this impact the way that we discipline?

    _____

    _____

    _____

3. How do you respond to Chip's statement that we are raising narcissists?

    _____

    _____

    _____

EFFECTIVE PARENTING IN A DEFECTIVE WORLD

4. Of the Four Ways to Use Words for Correction, which one most resonates with you as something you should focus on?

   _____

   _____

   _____

Live It Out – B.I.O.

BIO is a word that is synonymous with "life." Found in those three simple letters B.I.O., is the key to helping you become the person God wants you to be.

- B = Come **Before God** daily – To meet with Him personally through His word and prayer to enjoy His presence, receive His direction, and follow His will.

- I = Do Life **In Community** weekly – Structuring your week to personally connect in safe relationships that provide love, support, transparency, challenge, and accountability.

- O = Be **On Mission** 24/7 – Cultivating a mindset to "live out" Jesus' love for others through acts of sacrifice and service at home, work, play, and church.

Come Before God

5. Proverbs 13:24 (NIV) says, "Whoever spares the rod hates their children, but the one who loves their children is careful to discipline them."

   What do you think Solomon means by the phrase "whoever spares the rod hates their children"? And why does he use such strong language?

   _____

   _____

   _____

How to Discipline Your Child Effectively, Pt. 2

Do Life in Community

6. Being a parent in this generation is a huge challenge and can leave us feeling inadequate. You have now spent several weeks talking about raising godly kids. As you conclude this series, spend a few minutes affirming the other parents in the room. Where have you seen them grow? Where are they doing a great job with their kids? What do you appreciate about their parenting?

   _____

   _____

   _____

Be On Mission

7. This series has covered a lot of information. If you had to boil it down to the one most important "takeaway" for you as a parent, what would it be?

   _____

   _____

   _____

Small Group Leader Resources

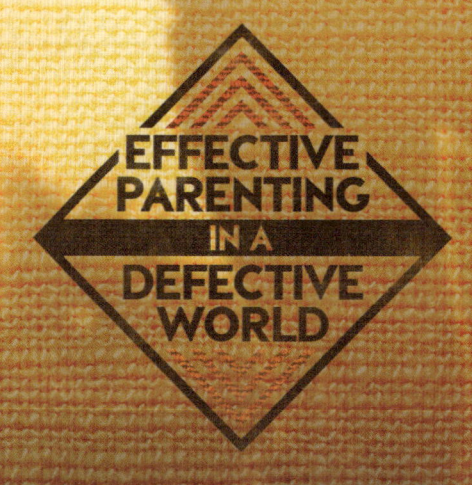

EFFECTIVE PARENTING IN A DEFECTIVE WORLD

Group Agreement

People come to groups with a variety of different expectations. The purpose of a group agreement is simply to make sure everyone is on the same page and that we have some common expectations.

The following Group Agreement is a tool to help you discuss specific guidelines during your first meeting. Modify anything that does not work for your group, then be sure to discuss the questions in the section called "Our Game Plan." This will help you to have an even greater group experience!

We Agree to the Following Priorities:

Take the Bible Seriously	To seek to understand and apply God's Truth in the Bible
Group Attendance	To give priority to the group meeting (call if I am going to be absent or late)
Safe Environment	To create a safe place where people can be heard and feel loved (no snap judgments or simple fixes)
Respectful Discussion	To speak in a respectful and honoring way to our mate and others in the group
Be Confidential	To keep anything that is shared strictly confidential and within the group
Spiritual Health	To give group members permission to help me live a godly, healthy spiritual life that is pleasing to God
Building Relationships	To get to know the other members of the group and pray for them regularly
Pursue B.I.O.	To encourage and challenge each other in "coming before God," "doing life together in community," and "being on mission 24/7"
Prayer	To regularly pray with and for each other
Other	_____

Help for Facilitating Your Group

Our Game Plan:

1. What day and time will we meet? _____

2. Where will we meet? _____

3. How long will we meet each week? _____

4. What will we do for refreshments? _____

5. What will we do about childcare? _____

Tips for Facilitating Your Group Meeting

Before the group arrives

1. BE PREPARED. Your personal preparation can make a huge difference in the quality of the group experience. We strongly suggest previewing both the DVD teaching by Chip Ingram and the study guide.

2. PRAY FOR YOUR GROUP MEMBERS BY NAME. Ask God to use your time together to touch the heart of every person in your group. Expect God to challenge and change people as a result of this study.

3. PROVIDE REFRESHMENTS. There's nothing like food to help a group relax and connect with each other. For the first week, we suggest you prepare a snack, but after that, ask other group members to bring the food so that they share in the responsibilities of the group and make a commitment to return.

4. RELAX. Don't try to imitate someone else's style of leading a group. Lead the group in a way that fits your style and temperament. Remember that people may feel nervous showing up for a small group study, so put them at ease when they arrive. Make sure to have all the details covered prior to your group meeting, so that once people start arriving, you can focus on them.

Take It In (Watch the Video)

1. GET THE VIDEO READY. Each video session will be between 30 and 35 minutes in length. Go ahead and cue up the video so that you can just push "play" when you are ready to watch the session.

2. HAVE AMPLE MATERIALS. Before you start the video, also make sure everyone has their own copy of the study guide. Encourage the group to open to this week's session and follow along with the teaching. There is an outline in the study guide with an opportunity to fill in the outline.

3. ARRANGE THE ROOM. Set up the chairs in the room so that everyone can see the television. And, arrange the room in such a way that it is conducive to discussion.

Talk It Over

Here are some guidelines for leading the discussion time:

1. MAKE THIS A DISCUSSION, not a lecture. Resist the temptation to do all the talking, and to answer your own questions. Don't be afraid of a few moments of silence while people formulate their answers.

   And don't feel like you need to have all the answers. There is nothing wrong with simply saying "I don't know the answer to that, but I'll see if I can find an answer this week."

2. ENCOURAGE EVERYONE TO PARTICIPATE. Don't let one person dominate, but also don't pressure quieter members to speak during the first couple of sessions. Be patient. Ask good follow up questions and be sensitive to delicate issues.

3. AFFIRM PEOPLE'S PARTICIPATION AND INPUT. If an answer is clearly wrong, ask "What led you to that conclusion?" or ask what the rest of the group thinks. If a disagreement arises, don't be too quick to shut it down! The discussion can draw out important perspectives, and if you can't resolve it there, suggest researching it further and return to the issue next week.

   However, if someone goes on the offensive and engages in personal attack, you will need to step in as the leader. In the midst of spirited discussion, we must also remember that people are fragile and there is no place for disrespect.

4. DETOUR WHEN NECESSARY. If an important question is raised that is not in the study guide, take time to discuss it. Also, if someone shares something personal and emotional, take time for them. Stop and pray for them right then. Allow the Holy Spirit room to maneuver, and follow His prompting when the discussion changes direction.

5. SUBGROUP. One of the principles of small group life is "when numbers go up, sharing goes down." So, if you have a large group, sometimes you may want to split up into groups of 4-6 for the discussion time. This is a

Help for Facilitating Your Group

great way to give everyone, even the quieter members, a chance to share. Choose someone in the group to guide each of the smaller groups through the discussion. This involves others in the leadership of the group, and provides an opportunity for training new leaders.

6. PRAYER. Be sensitive to the fact that some people in your group may be uncomfortable praying out loud. As a general rule, don't call on people to pray unless you have asked them ahead of time or have heard them pray in public. But this can also be a time to help people build their confidence to pray in a group. Consider having prayer times that ask people to just say a word or sentence of thanks to God.

Live It Out – B.I.O.

At this point in each week's session, you will engage the B.I.O. pathway. B.I.O. is a process that is designed to help Christians live like Christians. As you integrate these three vital practices into your life, it will result in spiritual momentum and help you thrive as a follower of Jesus.

- Come "BEFORE GOD" Daily - To meet with Him personally through His Word and prayer, in order to enjoy His Presence, receive His direction, and follow His will.

- Do Life "IN COMMUNITY" Weekly - Structuring your week to personally connect in safe relationships that provide love, support, transparency, challenge, and accountability.

- Be "ON MISSION" 24/7 - Cultivating a mindset to "live out" Jesus love for others through acts of sacrifice and service at home, work, play and church.

Accelerate (20 Minutes That Turn Concepts Into Convictions)

INSPIRATION comes from hearing God's Word; MOTIVATION grows by discussing God's Word; TRANSFORMATION occurs when you study it for yourself.

This 20 minute exercise is meant to be done apart from the group meeting. It is a great way to go deeper with the material and turbo charge people's growth. You can lead the way by personally doing the Accelerate section each week. And then encourage others to join and take a few moments in your group meeting to talk about what people have been learning from this section.

Effective Parenting in a Defective World Session Notes

Welcome to this series called *Effective Parenting in a Defective World*.

In this dynamic series Chip Ingram shares clear biblical teaching and years of practical experience as a parent. In these 8 sessions you are going to help lead your group to discover God's plan for raising godly children.

Whether you are brand new at leading a small group or you are a seasoned veteran, God is going to use you. God has a long history of using ordinary people to get His work done.

These brief notes are intended to help prepare you for each week's session. By spending just a few minutes each week previewing the video and going over these session notes you will set the table for a great group experience. Also, don't forget to pray for your group each week.

Session 1: How to Raise Positive Kids in a Negative World, Pt. 1

- If your group doesn't know each other well, be sure that you spend some time getting acquainted. Don't rush right into the video lesson. Remember, small groups are not just a study or a meeting, they are about relationships.

- If this is a new group, be sure to capture everyone's contact information. It is a good idea to send out an e-mail with everybody's contact information so that the group can stay in touch. At the back of your study guide is a roster where people can fill in the names and contact information of the other group members.

- When you are ready to start the session, be sure that each person in your group has a study guide. The small group study guide is important for people to follow along and to take notes.

- Spend a little time in this first session talking about B.I.O. These three core practices are the pathway to maturity. You will see these letters and terms throughout this curriculum. Start getting your group comfortable with the concepts of "coming Before God," "doing life together In Community," and "Being on Mission."

- Facilitating the discussion time, sometimes Chip will ask you, as the facilitator, to lead the way by answering the first question. This allows you to lead by example and your willingness to share openly about your life will help others feel the permission to do the same.

- During this session Chip will talk about having clear-cut objectives for parenting. In other words, we must be clear about the goal we are striving for. This is crucial to this entire series. Be sure to spend adequate time in your group meeting talking about this.

Session Notes

- One of the questions this week asks "If your goal truly became your child's "holiness" instead of their "happiness," how would that change your parenting?" This question challenges the conventional approach of our culture to parenting. So be prepared to give your answer to this question.

- Before you wrap up your group time in this first session, be sure to introduce the Accelerate exercise in the study guide. This is an assignment they can do during the week that will help turbo charge their growth as a parent. Encourage them to find a partner in the group who they can talk to each week about the Accelerate exercise.

Session 2: How to Raise Positive Kids in a Negative World, Pt. 2

- Why not begin your preparation by praying right now for the people in your group. You might even want to keep their names in your Bible. You may also want to ask people in your group how you can pray for them specifically.

- If somebody doesn't come back this week, be sure and follow up with them. Even if you knew they were going to have to miss the group meeting, give them a call or shoot them an e-mail letting them know that they were missed. It would also be appropriate to have a couple of other people in the group let them know they were missed.

- If you haven't already previewed the video, take the time to do so. It will help you know how to best facilitate the group and what are the best discussion questions for your group.

- Ask good follow up questions... the only thing better than a good question is a good follow up question. Think of your group discussion like an onion. Each good follow up question allows you to pull back another layer and get down beneath the surface.

- It would be easy during this series for people to feel very inadequate and to see all the ways that they are falling short as parents. Remind your group throughout this series that none of us parent perfectly and we are all on this journey together.

- One of the questions this week asks "What is one fun activity you could do with a friend and their kids that strengthen your relationship with your kids?" Don't just let this question be a brainstorming exercise. Challenge people to commit to something before leaving your small group meeting this week.

Session 3: How to Develop Your Child's Full Potential, Pt. 1

- Did anybody miss last week's session? If so, make it a priority to follow up and let them know they were missed. It just might be your care for them that keeps them connected to the group.

- Don't be afraid of silence. We don't like dead time, do we? It makes us feel uncomfortable. To be a good facilitator, you must learn to get comfortable with silence. Silence gives people a moment to process and figure out what they want to say. If you move on too quickly, you miss some of the best input.

- Think about last week's meeting for a moment. Was there anyone that didn't talk or participate? In every group there are extroverts and there are introverts. There are people who like to talk and then there are those who are quite content NOT to talk. Not everyone engages in the same way or at the same level but you do want to try and create an environment where everyone wants to participate.

- Follow up with your group this week to see how they did with the Accelerate assignment this week. Don't shame or embarrass anyone who didn't get to the assignment, but honestly challenge them to make this a priority in the coming week.

- Also, take a few moments to follow up on last week's challenge to do something fun with their kids to deepen the relational bond.

- The last thing you will do in your group meeting is spend some time praying for your kids. Be prepared to share specifically how the group can pray for your kids or for someone in your family.

Session 4: How to Develop Your Child's Full Potential, Pt. 2

- Don't feel any pressure to get through all the questions. As people open up and talk, don't move on too quickly. Give them the space to talk about what is going on inside them as they interact with this teaching.

- Share the load. One of the ways to raise the sense of ownership within the group is to get them involved in more than coming to the meeting. So, get someone to help with refreshments... find somebody else to be in charge of the prayer requests... get someone else to be in charge of any social gathering you plan... let someone else lead the discussion one night. Give away as much of the responsibility as possible. That is GOOD leadership.

- If your group is not sharing as much as you would like or if the discussion is being dominated by a person or two, try subgrouping. If your group is 8 people or more, this is a great way to up the level of participation. After

Session Notes

watching the video teaching, divide the group into a couple of smaller groups for the discussion time. It is good to get someone you think would be a good facilitator to agree to this ahead of time.

- Much of the emphasis in this session is about teaching our children to be responsible. Chip says that we should feed our kids responsibility like we feed them vitamins. This can be a huge challenge for some parents who tend to do most everything for their kids. Spend adequate time talking through this.

- At the end of your group time you will be asked the question "How can you help your kids to have a compassionate heart that cares for others?" You might want to consider doing a ministry project that involves all of the parents and kids in your small group.

Session 5: How to Prepare Your Kids to Win Life's Biggest Battles, Pt. 1

- You are now at the halfway point of this series. How is it going? How well is the group connecting? What has been going well and what needs a little work? Are there any adjustments you need to make?

- Confidentiality is crucial to group life. The moment trust is breached, people will shut down and close up. So, you may want to mention the importance of confidentiality again this week just to keep it on people's radar.

- Each time your group meets take a few minutes to update on what has happened since the last group meeting. Ask people what they are learning and putting into practice. Remember, being a disciple of Jesus means becoming a "doer of the Word."

- Revisit the importance of B.I.O. this week. Reinforce the importance of people integrating these core practices in their lives. For example, talk about the priority of coming before God each day and submitting to the authority of God's Truth.

- Don't chase rabbits. This happens in every group. You will ask a discussion question and someone will take you down a trail that really isn't relevant to the discussion. It is your job as the group leader to discern when you need to bring the group back. Here is how I often handle that situation... I will look for a moment to jump in and say "Hey, this is great discussion, but I want to come back to our topic and focus our discussion there."

- The first few questions in this week's session are about teaching your kids to manage their lives wisely... especially in the area of finances. This is, of course, not just an issue for kids. For some of the people in your small group, their finances might be a mess. First off, let the group know that they don't need to be doing it all perfectly to start teaching their kids. Secondly, challenge those in your group to start taking the steps to manage their own finances wisely.

- Another focal point of Chip's teaching this week is about teaching our kids to suffer well. As part of the discussion, the group will be asked to share a hard and painful experience from their life that God used to grow them. It might be helpful if you take the lead and share first.

Session 6: How to Prepare Your Kids to Win Life's Biggest Battles, Pt. 2

- One way to deepen the level of community within your group is to spend time together outside the group meeting. If you have not already done so, plan something that will allow you to get to know each other better. Also, consider having someone else in the group take responsibility for your fellowship event.

- As you begin this week's session, do a check-in to see what people are learning and applying from this series. Don't be afraid to take some time at the beginning of your meeting to review some key ideas from the previous week's lessons.

- Consider asking someone in your group to facilitate next week's lesson. Who knows, there might be a great potential small group leader in your group. It will give you a break and give them a chance to grow.

- Your job is not to lead a good meeting. Your job is to help develop those in your group into mature followers of Jesus. So, encourage people to take a next step in their growth. Don't just ask them what they could do, ask them what they WILL do. We don't grow by talking about obedience, we grow by "obeying" and being "doers of the Word."

- One of the things we can teach our kids is how to think biblically and critically. Chip will make this issue a focal point in his teaching this week. Help your group wrestle with the challenge of how we equip our kids with the truth of God's Word.

- This week Chip encourages us to monitor what goes into our child's mind. Have an honest discussion about how your group can be more proactive with this. You might even want to suggest families trying a media fast for a few days.

Session 7: How to Discipline Your Child Effectively, Pt. 1

- Since this is the next to the last week of this study, you might want to spend some time this week talking about what your group is going to do after

Session Notes

your complete this study. You might even consider having a computer available where your group can go to livingontheedge.org and explore other small group studies from Chip.

- Consider sending an e-mail to each person in your group this week letting them know you prayed for them today. Also, let them know that you are grateful that they are in the group.

- Take a few minutes this week before you get into the study to talk about the impact of this series so far. Ask people what they are learning, applying, and changing in their lives. For this series to have lasting impact, it has to be more than just absorbing information. So, challenge your group to put what they are learning into action.

- It is often a good idea to take a week break and do something different. This also helps the group understand that small group is more than just a meeting. You might consider taking one night off from your group meeting to just have dinner together and share/celebrate how God has used this series in your lives. Or, you could take a night off from your group meeting to do your ministry project and "do good" for someone in need.

- These last two sessions are about the topic of discipline. When you are in the middle of disciplining your kids, it is easy to lose sight of the end goal. So, at the end of this week's session your group will be asked to think ahead to the time when their kids are grown. And then they will be asked "What is the hope and longing you have for what discipline would have produced in their lives?"

Session 8: How to Discipline Your Child Effectively, Pt. 2

- "Thanks" for you willingness to lead this group... and thanks for your faithfulness in investing in those in your group. I hope you have grown and been blessed by this material and by the people in your group.

- Be sure that everyone is clear what the group is doing next after this study.

- This week's session will continue the discussion on discipline. And in this session Chip will address the controversial topic of spanking. As your group discusses this topic, be sure that it doesn't turn into a debate. It is fine for people to share their perspective but especially on this topic we must be gracious and allow people to hold different views from ours.

- As you conclude this series, your group will be encouraged to spend a few minutes affirming the other parents in the room. This can be a very meaningful time, so be sure to leave adequate time to do this exercise.

EFFECTIVE PARENTING IN A DEFECTIVE WORLD

- The last thing the group will be asked to do is to share the one most important takeaway from this series. Ask people to share the "one thing" they are committing to implement and work on as a parent.

Prayer and Praise

One of the most important things you can do in your group is to pray with and for each other. Write down each other's concerns here so you can remember to pray for these requests during the week!

Use the Follow Up box to record an answer to a prayer or to write down how you might want to follow up with the person making the request. This could be a phone call, an e-mail or a card. Your personal concern will mean a lot!

Date	Person	Prayer Request	Follow Up

EFFECTIVE PARENTING IN A DEFECTIVE WORLD

Date	Person	Prayer Request	Follow Up

Prayer and Praise

Date	Person	Prayer Request	Follow Up

EFFECTIVE PARENTING IN A DEFECTIVE WORLD

Date	Person	Prayer Request	Follow Up

Group Roster

Name	Home Phone	Email

EFFECTIVE PARENTING IN A DEFECTIVE WORLD

What's Next?
More Group Studies from Chip Ingram:

Balancing Life's Demands
Biblical Priorities for a Busy Life
Busy, tired and stressed out? Learn how to put "first things first" and find peace in the midst of pressure and adversity.

BIO
How to Become An Authentic Disciple of Jesus
Unlock the Biblical DNA for spiritual momentum by examining the questions at the heart of true spirituality.

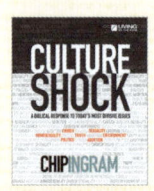

Culture Shock
A Biblical Response to Today's Most Divisive Issues
Bring light—not heat—to divisive issues, such as abortion, homosexuality, sex, politics, the environment, politics and more.

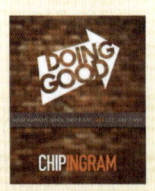

Doing Good
What Happens When Christians Really Live Like Christians
This series clarifies what Doing Good will do in you and then through you, for the benefit of others and the glory of God.

Experiencing God's Dream for Your Marriage
Practical Tools for a Thriving Marriage
Examine God's design for marriage and the real life tools and practices that will transform it for a lifetime.

Five Lies that Ruin Relationships
Building Truth-Based Relationships
Uncover five powerful lies that wreck relationships and experience the freedom of understanding how to recognize God's truth.

Watch previews and order at livingontheedge.org or 888.333.6003.

The Genius of Generosity
Lessons from a Secret Pact Between Friends
The smartest financial move you can make is to invest in God's Kingdom. Learn His design for wise giving and generous living.

Good to Great in God's Eyes
10 Practices Great Christians Have in Common
If you long for spiritual breakthrough, take a closer look at ten powerful practices that will rekindle a fresh infusion of faith.

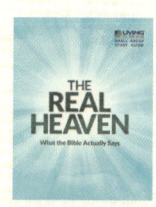

The Real Heaven
It's Not What You Think
Chip Ingram digs into scripture to reveal what heaven will be like, what we'll do there, and how we're to prepare for eternity today.

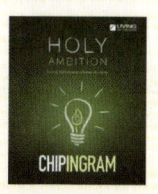

Holy Ambition
Turning God-Shaped Dreams Into Reality
Do you long to turn a God-inspired dream into reality? Learn how God uses everyday believers to accomplish extraordinary things.

House or Home: Marriage Edition
God's Blueprint for a Great Marriage
Get back to the blueprint and examine God's plan for marriages that last for a lifetime.

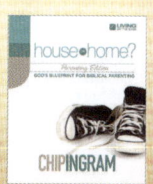

House or Home: Parenting Edition
God's Blueprint for Biblical Parenting
Timeless truths about God's blueprint for parenting, and the potential to forever change the trajectory of your family.

What's Next?
More Group Studies from Chip Ingram:

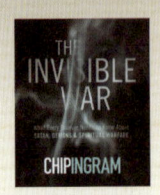

The Invisible War
The Believer's Guide to Satan, Demons and Spiritual Warfare
Learn how to clothe yourself with God's "spiritual armor" and be confident of victory over the enemy of your soul.

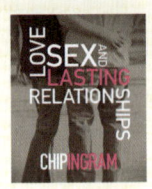

Love, Sex and Lasting Relationships `UPDATED`
God's Prescription to Enhance Your Love Life
Do you believe in "true love"? Discover a better way to find love, stay in love, and build intimacy that lasts a lifetime.

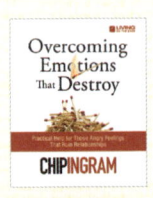

Overcoming Emotions that Destroy
Constructive Tools for Destructive Emotions
We all struggle with destructive emotions that can ruin relationships. Learn God's plan to overcome angry feelings for good.

Rebuilding Your Broken World
How God Puts Broken Lives Back Together
Learn how God can reshape your response to trials and bring healing to broken relationships and difficult circumstances.

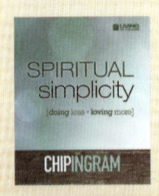

Spiritual Simplicity
Doing Less · Loving More
If you crave simplicity and yearn for peace this study is for you. Spiritual simplicity can only occur when we do less and love more.

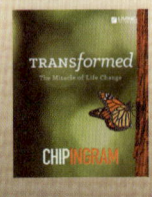

Transformed
The Miracle of Life Change
Ready to make a change? Explore God's process of true transformation and learn to spot barriers that hold you back from receiving God's best.

Watch previews and order at **livingontheedge.org** or **888.333.6003.**

True Spirituality
Becoming a Romans 12 Christian
We live in a world that is activity-heavy and relationship-light. Learn the next steps toward True Spirituality.

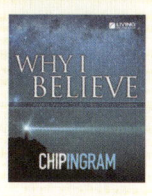

Why I Believe
Answers to Life's Most Difficult Questions
Can miracles be explained? Is there really a God? There are solid, logical answers about claims of the Christian faith.

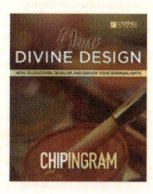

Your Divine Design
Discover, Develop and Deploy Your Spiritual Gifts
How has God uniquely wired you? Discover God's purpose for spiritual gifts and how to identify your own.

Download the Chip Ingram App

The Chip Ingram App delivers daily devotionals, broadcasts, message notes, blog articles and more right on your mobile device.

- Get it on iTunes
- ANDROID APP ON Google play
- Download from Windows Phone Store
- amazon apps Available on kindle fire

89